D1442332

Cartooning for Kids!

Space Aliens

By Dave Garbot

This library edition published in 2016 by Walter Foster Jr.,
an imprint of Quarto Publishing Group USA Inc.
6 Orchard Road, Suite 100
Lake Forest, CA 92630

Distributed in the United States and Canada by
Lerner Publisher Services
241 First Avenue North
Minneapolis, MN 55401 U.S.A.
www.lernerbooks.com

First Library Edition

Library of Congress Cataloging-in-Publication Data

Garbot, Dave, author, illustrator.
  Space aliens / By Dave Garbot. -- First Library Edition.
      pages cm. -- (Cartooning for kids!)
  "Illustrated and written by Dave Garbot."
  ISBN 978-1-939581-94-5
1. Science fiction--Illustrations--Juvenile literature. 2. Extraterrestrial beings in art--Juvenile
literature. 3. Cartoon characters in art--Juvenile literature. 4. Drawing--Technique--Juvenile
literature. I. Title.
  NC825.S34G37 2015
  741.5'1--dc23
                                                            2015031681

9 8 7 6 5 4 3 2 1

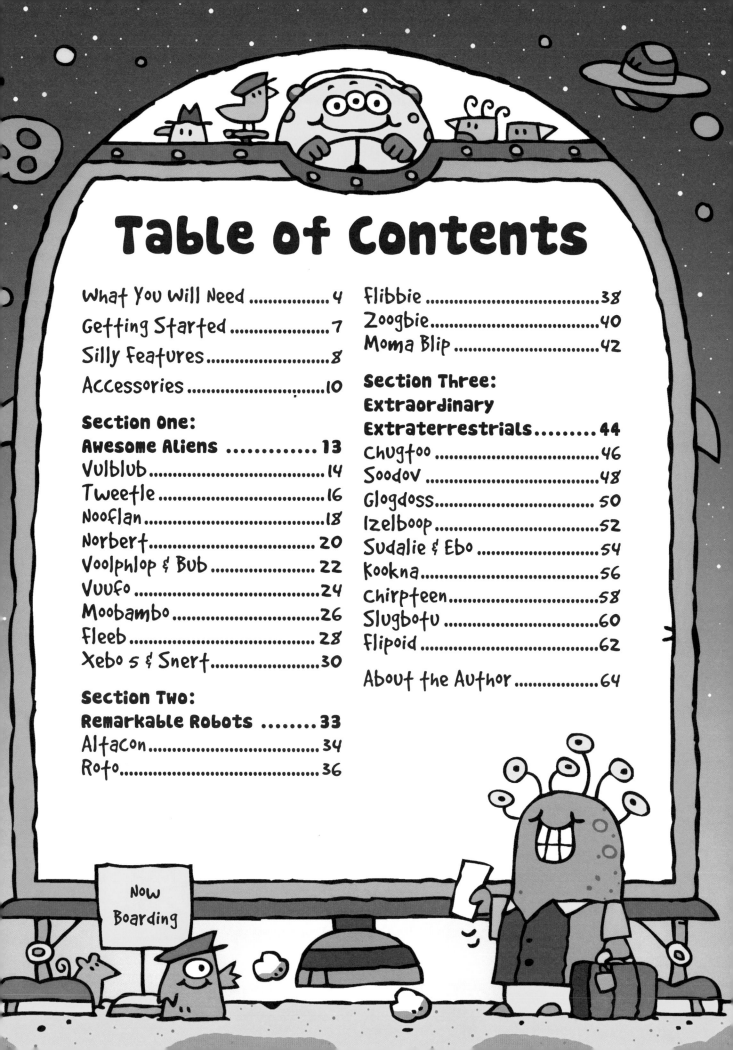

Table of Contents

What You Will Need

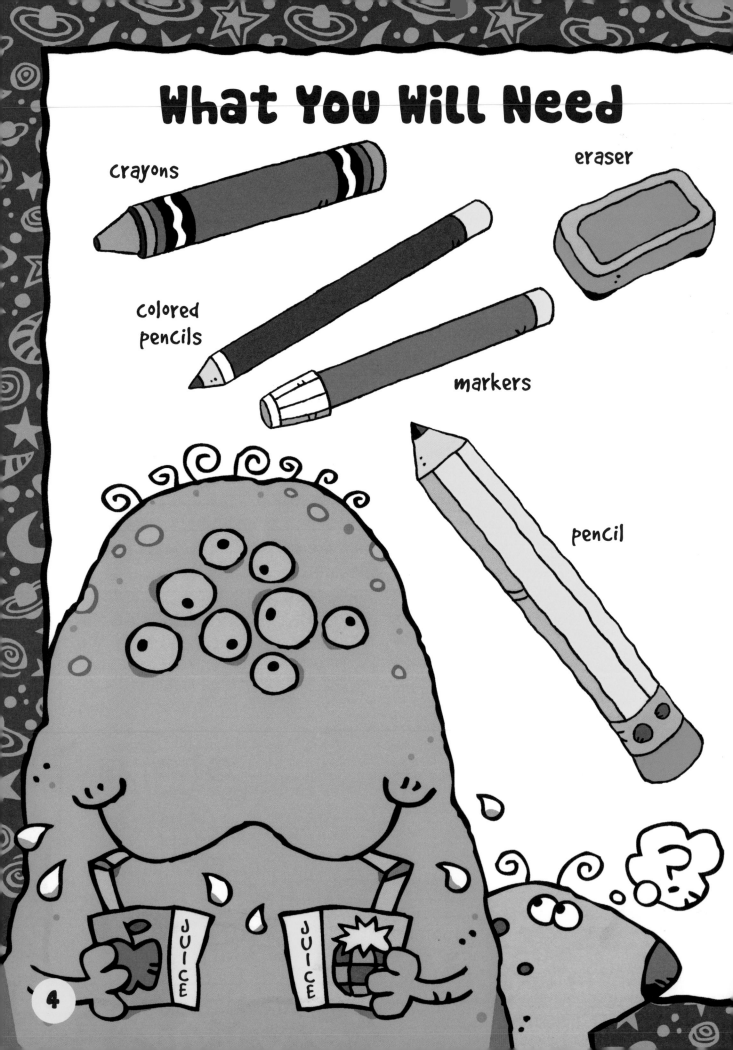

crayons

eraser

colored pencils

markers

pencil

4

Drawing paper

Getting Started

Now that we have everything we need, we're ready to draw some out-of-this-world creatures! Some will have five eyes, and some will have only one! You never know with aliens because they're all so different, which makes them a lot of fun to draw! So grab your pencil and maybe a cookie or two (because aliens really love cookies), and let's see what kind of kooky extraterrestrials we can create!

Silly Features

Here are a few things you can use when drawing your aliens. Maybe you'll want different eyes, a silly mouth, or crazy ears. Come back to this page anytime, and Sparky can help you with some ideas.

Features Dept.

Accessories

Aliens are a very weird group. You never know what they'll walk around with or wear! You might want them to hold a fish, a mop, or even a taco! Come back here any time you need accessory ideas!

Awesome Aliens

Our first group of projects is all lined up and ready for takeoff! Anything goes with these creatures, so maybe you can add a few accessories to really bring out their awesomeness!

13

VULBLUB

Do you think this alien needs more fish in his bubble? Fewer?
Can you add anything else? How about a pizza slice
or an ice cream cone?

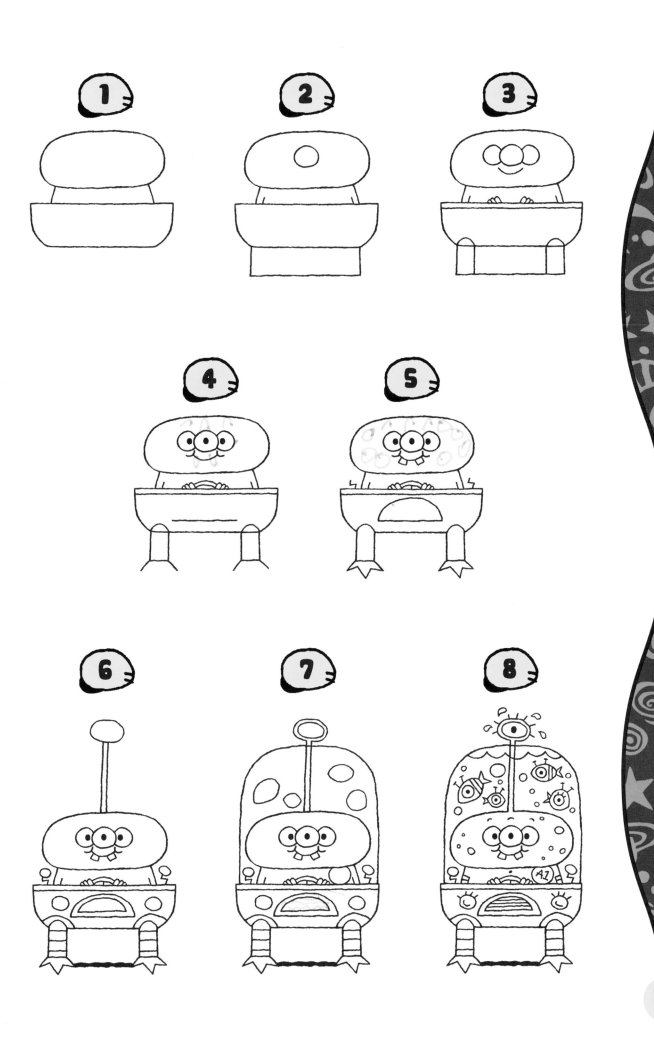

Tweetle

Try drawing this alien a second time without his legs, and he'll look like he's flying!

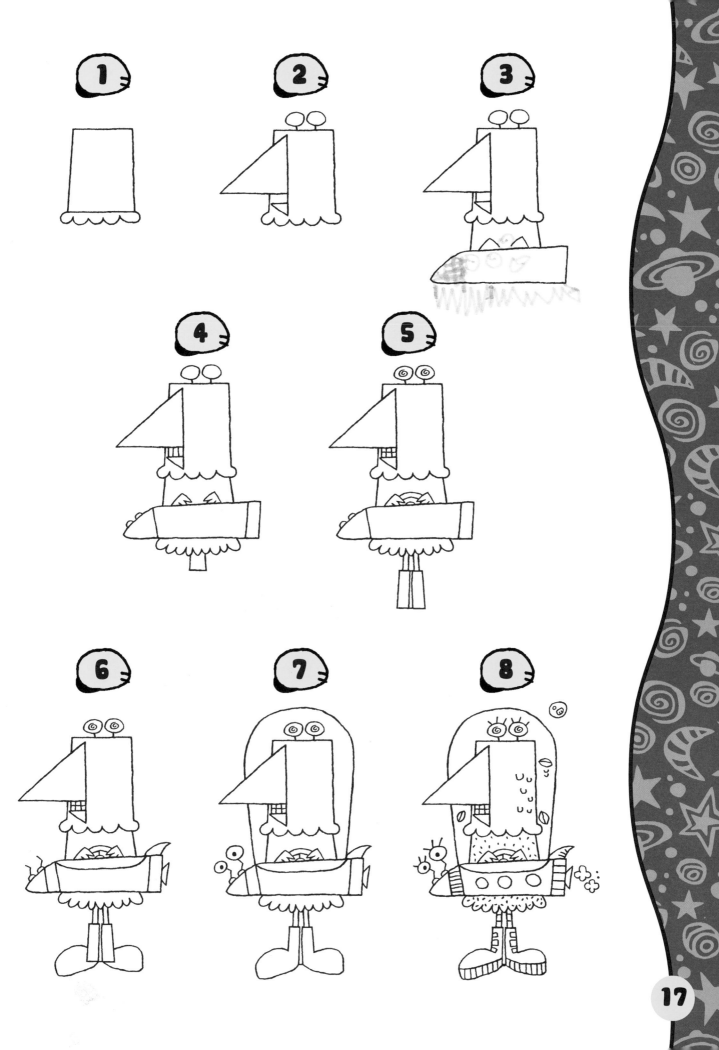

Nooflan

This alien has a green carrot on top of his space bubble. Can you think of something else to draw instead? How about a banana, a fish, or maybe a pickle?

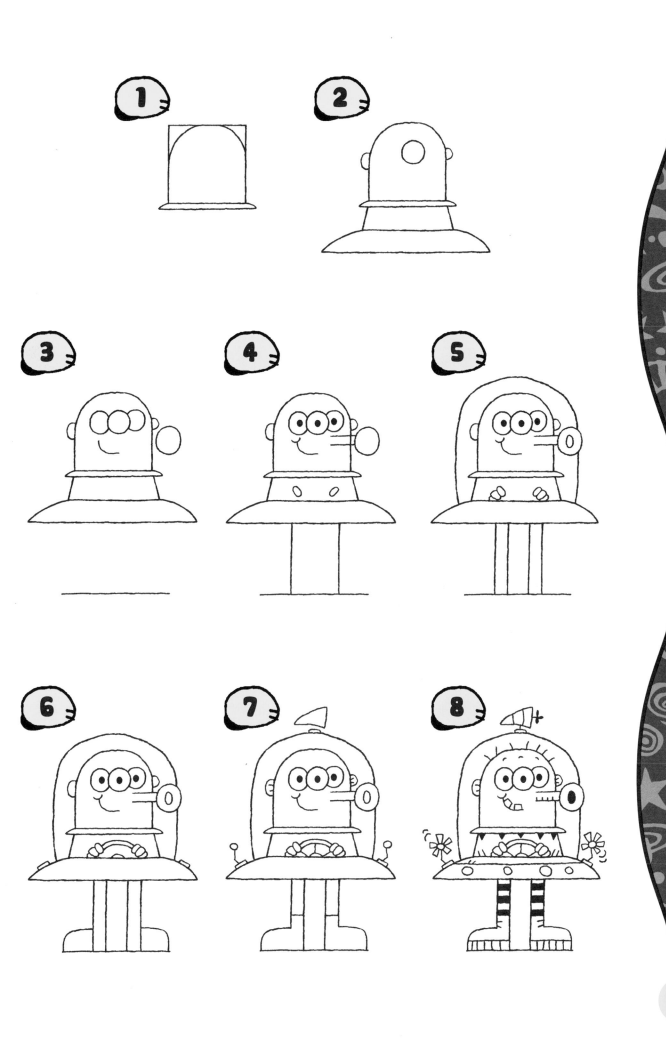

Norbert

The lower you draw the shadow under the spaceship, the higher it will seem to be flying! In step 1, start out with a simple square, but round the top edge just a little bit.

Voolphlop & Bub

Can you give this alien a hat to go with her purse? Check page 10 for ideas. Adding twinkle marks around the antennae will help give your drawing a little more sparkle!

Vuufo

This alien looks pretty serious. How can you make him look happier? Try adding more Space Birds to the scene. Can you draw one on top of Vuufo's helmet?

Moobambo

How would he look with no arms and more eyes?
Try making the eyeballs different sizes!

Fleeb

Fleeb has five eyes! How would he look with one big eye instead? How about one tiny one? Don't worry too much about the shape of his head—it should look like a big blob, or a potato!

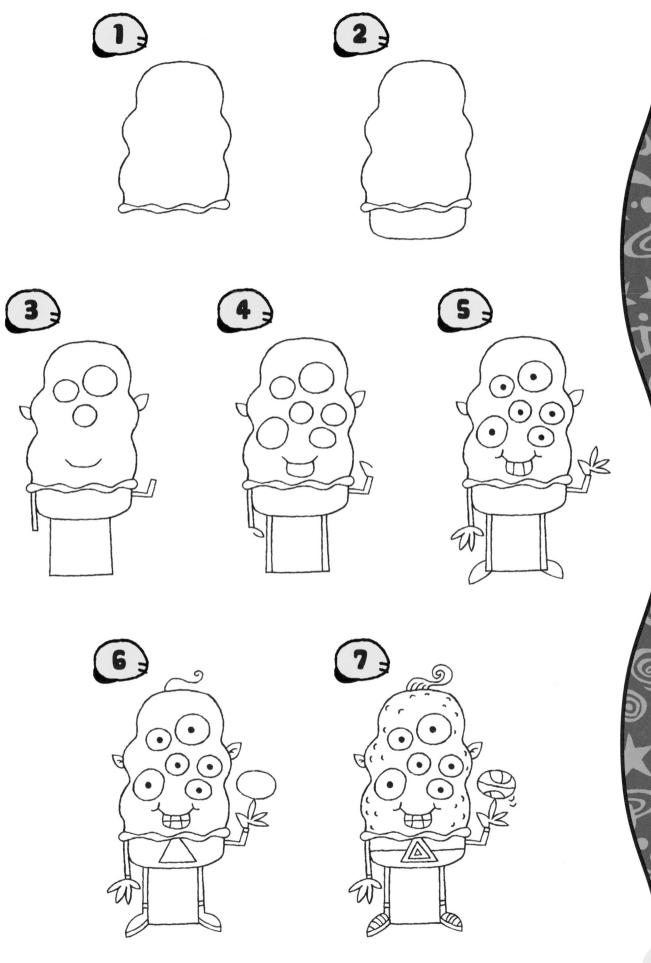

Xebo 5 & Snert

This is a crazy pair! Can you give Xebo 5 a few more ears and another mouth? How about an extra tail for Snert?

Section Two

Remarkable Robots

In this section we'll draw aliens that are put together with a few nuts, bolts, and wires! That might seem strange, but not if you're an alien ROBOT! Have fun drawing this group, and don't forget... they like ice cream!

Altacon

This Robo alien is blasting off! Try drawing the groundline even lower to make him look like he's high in the air!

Roto

Can you give this alien a funny hat instead of his propeller?
How would this alien look with three eyes or different ears?
Go back to page 8 if you need some ideas!

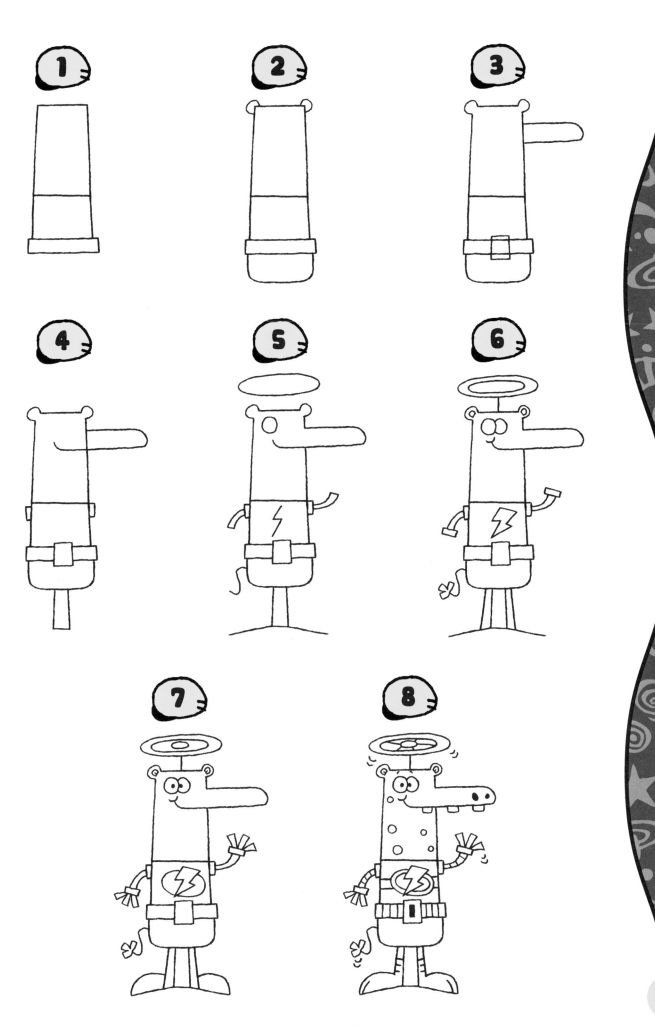

Flibbie

Do you think flibbie needs a hat? Check out page 10 if you need an idea!

Zoogbie

This alien loves pizza, but can you think of something else he might want to juggle instead? Check the accessories page if you need ideas!

41

MoMa Blip

How would this alien look without her helmet? Can you make more mini aliens for MoMa Blip to keep track of?

Extraordinary Extraterrestrials

You never know where aliens will show up. For this group it's another day at the beach, but maybe they'll appear at school, in the playground, or even in your backyard! Think about where your characters like to hang out, and add that place to your drawing!

Chugtoo

This alien has some crazy feet. Can you make them bigger or smaller? How about giving him some crazy shoes instead?

Soodov

Try drawing this alien with more teeth or another eye or two ... or three!

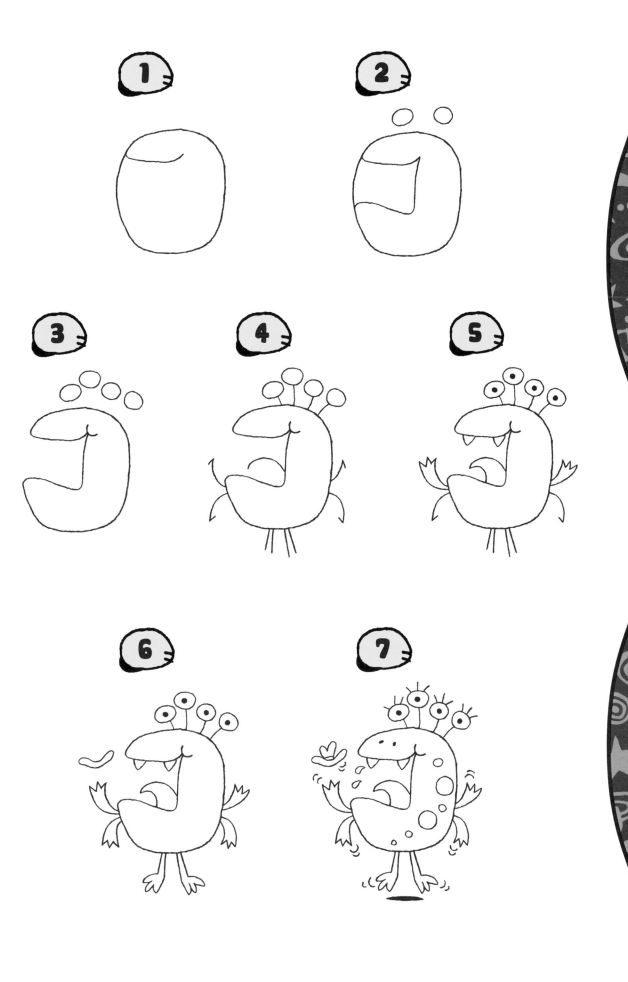

Glogdoss

Can you make this creature another color? How would he look with a smaller eye? How about a much bigger eye?

Izelboop

Can you add a silly hat to this pizza girl? In step 7, try changing this alien's mouth. Go to page 8 if you need an idea.

Sudalie & Ebo

These two aliens look happy sitting on a bench, but can you draw them standing? How would you draw their feet?

Kookna

This is a kooky-looking alien! How would he look with sunglasses? After you've drawn this alien, try drawing another one, but really BIG!

Chirpteen

Can you add more of the little bird creatures to this drawing? What if one or two were upside down?

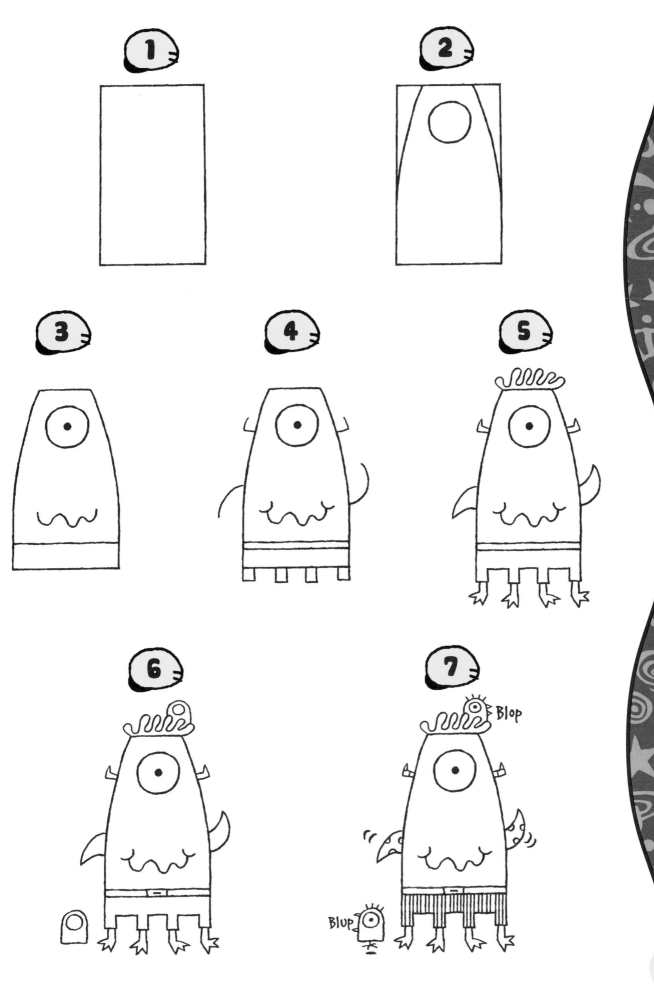

Blop

Blup

Slugbotu

Six eyes, but only two arms? How would he look with another pair of arms? How about another mouth or two? This alien is like a worm, so your lines can be extra wiggly if you want!

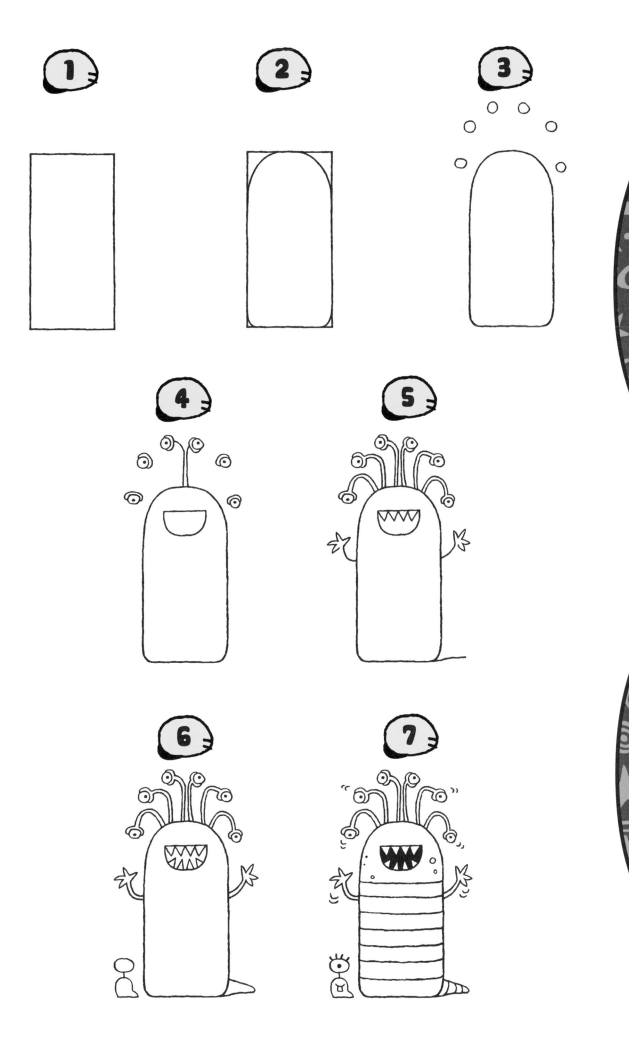

Flipoid

This wacky alien has a carrot in his pocket. How about drawing a banana, an ice cream cone, or a fish instead? Adding a groundline and motion lines by his flippers will make him look like he's jiggling!

About the Author

Dave Garbot is a professional illustrator and has been drawing for as long as he can remember. He is frequently called upon to create characters for children's books and other publications. Dave always has a sketchbook with him, and he gets many of his ideas from the things he observes every day as well as from lots of colorful childhood memories. Although he admits that creating characters brings him personal enjoyment, making his audience smile, feel good, and maybe even giggle is what really makes his day.

Dave is from Portland, Oregon, and you can see more of his work at www.garbot.com.